I SPY
MERRY CHRISTMAS

Riddles by Jean Marzollo
Photographs by Walter Wick

I Spy Santa Claus
and
I Spy a Candy Cane

SCHOLASTIC INC.

I Spy Santa Claus (ISBN-10: 0-439-78414-X)
Text copyright © 2005 by Jean Marzollo.
Photographs copyright © 1992 by Walter Wick.

I Spy a Candy Cane (ISBN-10: 0-439-52474-1)
Text copyright © 2004 by Jean Marzollo.
Photographs copyright © 1992 by Walter Wick.

All images by Walter Wick taken from *I Spy Christmas*.
Published by Scholastic Inc. in 1992.

ISBN-13: 978-0-545-03945-1
ISBN-10: 0-545-03945-2

18 17 16 15 14   23/0

Printed in the U.S.A. 40 • This edition first printing, August 2008

I Spy Santa Claus

Remembering with love,
Mr. Christmas,
Freddy Faust
(1947–2005)
—J.M.

For Edward Emilio Vidal
—W.W.

I Spy a Candy Cane

For Dave and Brian with thanks to Dan
—J.M.

For Linda
—W.W.

I SPY
SANTA CLAUS

Riddles by Jean Marzollo
Photographs by Walter Wick

I spy

a belt,

 a bell that's blue,

a teddy bear's bow,

and a butterfly, too.

I spy

an umbrella,

yarn that's pink,

Santa on skis,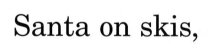

and a nice warm drink.

I spy

a dog,

 a marble that's red,

a Santa cap bear,

and a heart-shaped head.

I spy

 two horses,

a cookie O,

 a purple squirrel,

and a star's yellow glow.

I spy

a white horse,

 a 7,

two socks,

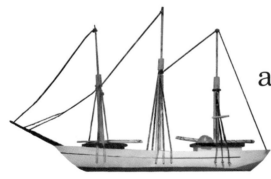 a sailing ship,

and a furry white fox.

I spy

a trumpet,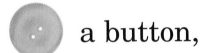

 a button,

a jack,

 a bearded face,

and a nose that's black.

I spy

a carrot,

 the number 8,

a bear on a drum,

 and a roller skate.

I spy

 glasses,

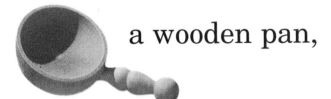 a wooden pan,

an empty heart,

 and a big policeman.

I spy

a dog,

 twin birds,

a fish,

 a toothy grin,

and a star for a wish.

I spy

 a rooster,

Santa in the sky,

a gift,

and an angel ready to fly.

I spy two matching words.

 Santa cap bear

two socks

Santa in the sky

I spy two matching words.

dog

dog

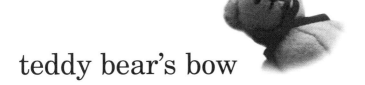

teddy bear's bow

I spy two words that start with the letter P.

big policeman

 yarn that's pink

cookie O

I spy two words that start
with the letters GL.

glasses

sailing ship

star's yellow glow

I spy two words that end with the letter T.

trumpet

 carrot

furry white fox

I spy two words that end
with the letters EL.

 purple squirrel

jack

 angel ready to fly

I spy two words that rhyme.

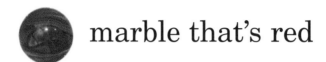 marble that's red

 fish

heart-shaped head

I spy two words that rhyme.

 two horses

bell that's blue

 gift

I SPY

A CANDY CANE

Riddles by Jean Marzollo
Photographs by Walter Wick

I spy

 a red roof,

eight reindeer,

 a Y,

a French horn,

 an apple,

and a bright blue fly.

I spy  a horse,

three gumdrops,

a J,

a rope,

and a sock that's
red and gray.

I spy

 two candles meant
for a cake,

two golden bells,

 and a pretty snowflake.

I spy

a flag,

 a tiny yellow bear,

an ice-cream cone,

 and a face with
white hair.

I spy

 a mallet,

a cookie-cutter tree,

 strawberry leaves,

and some cherries for me.

I spy

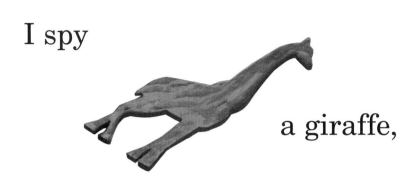 a giraffe,

a gift box,

 a king,

a green paint jar,

and popcorn string.

I spy

 a 4,

a blanket,

 a steeple,

a tiara,

 and a bus for tiny people.

I spy

a candle,

 a snake,

a 2,

 a shiny moon,

and a sleigh that's blue.

I spy

a snowman,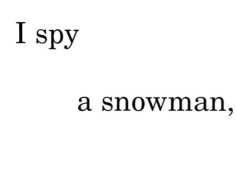

 a horn,

a key,

 a spider's web,

and an icicle tree.

I spy

a drum,

a zebra's mane,

 a man with
a tree,

and a candy cane.

I spy 2 matching words.

red roof

 eight reindeer

sock that's red
and gray

I spy 2 matching words.

 man with
a tree

two golden bells

 face with white hair

I spy 2 words that start with the letter G.

giraffe

three gumdrops

 a bright blue fly

I spy 2 words that start with the letters ST.

strawberry leaves

 a king

steeple

I spy 2 words that end
with the letter Y.

a candle

 bus for tiny people

candy cane

I spy 2 words that end with the letter R.

 eight reindeer

bear

 a horn

I spy 2 words that rhyme.

two candles
meant for a cake

snake

mallet

I spy 2 words that rhyme.

key

 a flag

icicle tree